Myth Quest
Mahishasura

THE BUFFALO DEMON

retold by Anu Kumar

illustrations by Amir Khan

First published in 2012 by Hachette India
(Registered name: Hachette Book Publishing India Pvt. Ltd)
An Hachette UK company
www.hachetteindia.com

SRD

ISBN 978-93-5009-535-5

Hachette Book Publishing India Pvt Ltd,
4th & 5th Floors, Corporate Centre;
Plot No. 94, Sector 44; Gurgaon 122003, India

Typeset in Adobe Garamond Pro 13/16
by Eleven Arts, New Delhi

Printed and bound in India by
Manipal Technologies Limited, Manipal

Welcome to the world of MythQuest . . .

Discover the fables and legends about the origin, history, deities, ancestors and heroes of India.

While the term 'myth' in common conversation means a false story, in the world of religion, folklore and magic, myths are considered 'true'. They tell stories of the creation of the universe, the eternal battle between good and evil and the history of humankind itself.

The main characters in our myths are bigger and better than any modern superheroes. They are birds and beasts, asuras *and gods, kings and queens, generals and warriors, sages and gurus, each with extraordinary powers that changed the course of history and the fate of the human race.*

The people to whom a myth belongs consider it as a true account of their past millions of years ago. Even today, they continue to worship the gods and goddesses, follow the rituals and read the texts that developed from these myths.

Hachette India's MythQuest series brings to you fascinating stories from the vast treasures of ancient mythology. Read them all—become a MythMaster!

Mythological characters and events have been described in different ways in different versions of ancient texts. We have chosen the most interesting and key stories to build a comprehensive account for the young reader.

This story is about . . .

Mahishasura, a terrible and greatly feared asura, *or demon. Mahishasura could assume the form of a powerful buffalo at will and thus he is referred to as Mahishasura, or the buffalo demon. Mahisha is the Sanskrit word for buffalo.*

Mahishasura was blessed with great powers due to a boon from Lord Brahma. The asura *was finally killed by the Goddess Durga, a manifestation of* shakti, *born of the combined powers of all the gods. It was only Goddess Durga with her unique powers and abilities who could override Lord Brahma's boon and save the universe from this demon's evil ways. Goddess Durga is therefore worshipped as 'Mahishamardini' or the slayer of Mahishasura. Goddess Durga's victory symbolises the triumph of good over evil.*

The myth of Mahishasura Mardini is found in several Puranas including the Kalika Purana, the Vamana Purana, the Varaha Purana, the Shiva Purana, the Skanda Purana, the Markandeya Purana and the Devi Bhagwati Purana.

According to one tribe in North Bengal, Mahishasura is believed to be their forefather. Their surname is asura *and the five days of Durga Puja which is traditionally celebrated as a time of celebration for the killing of Mahishasura is a period of mourning for them.*

Read about Mahishasura's strange birth, his unmatched power, the terrible wars and finally, his violent end at the hands of Goddess Durga . . .

CHAPTER ONE

A GREAT PENANCE AND A FIERY BIRTH

A long time ago there was an asura called Dhanu. Dhanu had two sons, Rambha and Karambha. Rambha was king of the *asuras*. He ruled over the underworld as well as all the dark and fearful places on earth. Rambha was a cruel king, who always tormented and troubled his subjects.

Both Rambha and Karambha wanted to acquire even greater powers and so they decided to offer prayers and immerse themselves in long years of austerities, seeking the blessings of the most powerful gods.

Karambha was a gigantic *asura* and so he went to the

deepest lake there was in the three worlds. Once there, he sank into its immense depths till the waters covered him up to the neck. Rambha, not to be outdone, stepped into a great fire that had burnt brightly over days and months and years and still showed no signs of abating.

Thus settled in their extremely difficult positions, the two brothers began their meditation. The intensity of their penance worried the gods immensely as they thought that such intense meditation and penance could give the *asura* brothers powers that might rival those of the gods themselves.

Indra, the King of the Gods and Lord of Heaven, foresaw the danger that Rambha and Karambha posed to the divine beings and decided to take matters into his own hands. Thus, Lord Indra took on the form of a ferocious crocodile and swam into the deep lake where Karambha meditated. In such a form, the Lord of Heaven attacked Karambha who was deep in his meditation and oblivious to the physical world around him. Karambha was so focussed on his penance that he was caught entirely unawares by the giant crocodile. Before he could put up any resistance, the crocodile mauled, bit and tore the *asura's* flesh. The duel was over in no time as Karambha died instantly.

Although Rambha was in deep meditation, he was informed of his brother's death. Now Rambha loved his brother dearly, and felt totally helpless at being unable to save him, or help him in his last moments. He lost all desire to live and contemplated taking his own life. He missed Karambha terribly but was also filled with a deep anger at the cowardly manner in which his brother had been killed.

Having already acquired powers from his penance, Rambha willed the flames around him to rise higher. The fire spread fast and quickly across the three worlds. This scared the gods terribly as they feared that the heat of this cursed fire would consume Heaven itself.

In desperation, the gods appealed to Agni, the God of Fire, to intervene. Lord Agni appeared before Rambha and asked him to end his penance, promising in turn to grant him whatever boon he wished for. Rambha, deeply distressed at losing his brother, and bursting with revenge, asked for a son who would become so powerful that he would rule all the three worlds. He asked for a son who would be invincible against the gods and have extreme skill in all kinds of weaponry. Finally, he prayed that his son should have the ability for instantaneous transformation into a variety of forms.

Even though this was a great boon, Lord Agni agreed to grant it as the whole universe was in danger of being consumed by Rambha's vengeful fire.

Thus having been blessed by Lord Agni, Rambha returned to his kingdom with greater powers than before.

One day, Rambha spotted a beautiful water buffalo while out on a hunt. Now this was no ordinary buffalo, and was in fact a beautiful princess called Shyamala who had been cursed. Rambha fell in love with her instantly and transformed himself into a male buffalo. In this form, he began wooing her with great passion and persistence. Shyamala could not resist the attention and also fell in love with him. But another male buffalo noticed this and could not hold back his jealousy. Rambha and Shyamala were so engrossed in each other that they did not notice the jealous rival who crept up behind Rambha.

The jealous male attacked the disguised *asura* king viciously and gored him to death. The grief-stricken she-buffalo also gave up her life by jumping into the huge funeral pyre that was lit for Rambha.

But a god's boon that is granted does not go in vain. Therefore a baby boy was born from the funeral fire of Rambha and the water buffalo. In time, the boy came to be known as Mahishasura. Due to his strange birth, Mahishasura was born with the ability to change his form effortlessly from a human being to a buffalo.

CHAPTER TWO

THE BOON OF INVINCIBILITY

After the death of Rambha, Mahishasura was brought up by his relatives. In due course, he became king and the kingdom he ruled over was called Mahisha. Mahishasura soon distinguished himself as a formidable and uncompromising general and following the footsteps of his father, he established himself as a major enemy of the *devas*, or gods.

Renowned demon heroes like Tikshur, Tamra, Asiloma, Sudarka, Vidal, Trinetra and Kalavandhaka became his ministers and generals. He ruled over an even larger area than his father, for he was brave and courageous and above all a brilliant general. Most times, when threatened by a strong enemy, he led his armies by simply taking on the form of a buffalo. In this way, he effortlessly demolished fort walls or gored through well-built chariots and ran down mighty elephants and fleet-footed horses.

The war between the *devas* and the *asuras* continued for a long, long time. Mahishasura too wanted special powers like his father and uncle. Having learnt about how he was born and the manner in which his father and uncle had been killed, he longed for a way to trounce the gods and humiliate them.

So he decided to turn to Lord Brahma, one of the most powerful gods and the Creator of the Universe. He knew that whoever propitiated the almighty trinity of Brahma, Vishnu and Shiva, would never be turned away empty-handed.

So he set himself the task of winning Lord Brahma's attention. He decided to undertake a great penance, for he knew that any boon granted to him by Lord Brahma would be lasting and its effects would have a deep impact.

His mind thus made up, he began his meditation chanting Lord Brahma's name over and over. His austerities lasted for long and seemingly unending years. He was undisturbed by rain, the sun's heat, or even terribly cold winters. Nothing ruffled his concentration.

And after many years, Lord Brahma had no option but to appear before this great devotee.

Lord Brahma appeared sitting on his lotus, his four heads keeping an eye on the four cardinal points, and commanded Mahishasura to end his penance.

'I am pleased with your effort, O *asura* king. Ask me what you want,' said Lord Brahma. 'And I will see if I grant it, within my limitations.'

The *asura* opened his eyes and blinked. The blinding halo of light that surrounded Brahma was hard to bear. He bowed low and was profuse in his thanks.

'It is very kind of you, O Supreme God to appear before me for I know how many matters of the universe you have to attend to.'

'Speak,' commanded Lord Brahma, his heads turning this way and that, as the universe created itself around him every moment.

'My Lord Brahma, no doubt you know how great my father Rambha and even my uncle Karambha were. I too wish for special powers like theirs so that I may fulfil the many tasks they left incomplete. O Lord, grant me that I should be immortal for all time to come.'

Lord Brahma heard him out with a grim look on his face. 'Unfortunately, I cannot grant you that, O *asura*! Whoever is born must die. That is the rule of the universe and I cannot make you immortal. Ask me for some other boon,' said Brahma.

'Grant me then, O Lord, that no hero among the gods or men can ever vanquish me,' prayed Mahishasura.

Brahma hesitated, but only just. In his wisdom, he realised what the *asura* was getting at. But he knew he could not simply turn down everything the *asura* asked. After all, he had spent long years in penance and had performed every kind of austerity and he deserved his boon.

So he nodded, and in his all-knowing way intoned, 'I know what your father would have wanted. He too spent years engaged in the same austerities that you just performed. So I grant you a boon that would have made him very happy. I grant you, O Mahishasura, born of buffalo and man, the boon that will make you invincible in any battle you fight with man or god.'

Mahishasura bowed low in gratitude. He was very grateful. He did not care to explore any loopholes in Lord Brahma's boon, and that was what led to his undoing later.

CHAPTER THREE

A REIGN OF TERROR

Filled with happiness after receiving this great boon from Lord Brahma, Mahishasura then retraced his steps back to his kingdom. As news of the *asura* king's new-found powers spread in his kingdom, his subjects trembled in fear. Mahishasura had grown even taller, stronger and more powerful after the years spent meditating and gods, sages and ordinary human beings knew that this could not bode well for them.

Mahishasura made his intentions known the very moment he reached his kingdom. He let loose a reign of tyranny, throwing caution to the wind, uncaring as to who he offended. No longer did he worry about the wrath of the gods, or the curses of the holy men.

His army of *asuras* attacked, plundered and destroyed mercilessly, and he himself led them in battles against every kingdom on earth.

The ground shuddered under his feet, trees shrivelled and animals and birds scurried away from his path. Mahishasura was on a rampage. Undefeated, he waged wars and expanded his kingdom over the universe. The fear spread far and wide and only seemed to grow with each passing day.

Sometimes when the army came up with unexpected resistance, or when the soldiers of the opposing camp put up a brave fight, Mahishasura led from the front. Since he could change himself into a buffalo at will, he did so whenever the need arose. In the form of a fearsome black buffalo, the great *asura* would charge ahead. The buffalo demon was a fearsome sight indeed with smoke bellowing out from his nostrils, his cries echoing through the skies and his hooves churning so much dust, that the entire universe was covered by clouds of evil brown smog.

He would jump across the sky, taking a huge leap over mountains that rose as obstacles in his path. He would grow larger and larger and leap across planets that came in his way. In this way, hollering, shouting and brandishing a heavy club, he finally led his *asura* army to the very gates of Heaven.

Bursting with confidence and arrogance, he sent a messenger to Lord Indra, challenging his supremacy and inviting him to battle. The King of Gods anticipating this attack, had already ordered for the heavenly gates to be bolted and fortified against the invaders. His soldiers stood at the ramparts ready to pour boiling oil on the hordes of *asuras*.

Unfortunately, none of this had any effect. Mahishasura's powers were bolstered by his years of

prayer and strengthened by the boon granted by Lord Brahma. He rushed at the tall, imposing walls, ready to take on the army of gods.

Once again assuming his buffalo form, he charged forward, his head lowered, his horns curved and menacing, symbolizing destruction.

The walls of Heaven were no match for the all-mighty blows of Mahishasura's gigantic horns. The gods trembled in fear as they heard his furious snorting and saw the smoke emanating from his nostrils.

Even Lord Indra's Vajra, or thunderbolt, was no match for Mahishasura's hoof, horn, tail and fiery breath. Apart from his buffalo form, the asura king also had the ability to transform into a powerful lion.

Mahishasura's army fought for a hundred years with the gods. But finally, the *devas* were defeated and fled for their safety. They rode away in their chariots and on their *vahanas*, or vehicles, flying through the sky at breakneck speed. Mahishasura thus became the lord of Heaven and occupied the beautiful throne of Lord Indra.

CHAPTER FOUR

THE DIVINE TRINITY TO THE RESCUE

Once they had been defeated in battle and forced to abandon their abode, the gods approached Lord Brahma. Led by their king, Lord Indra, the gods appealed to Lord Brahma to do something to help them. However, the Creator of the Universe sat impassive and finally spread his hands wide to show his helplessness.

'I know that you are in great trouble because of my boon, but unfortunately, I cannot do anything about it,' he said. 'The powers granted by a boon cannot be revoked under any circumstances.'

Lord Brahma's words were greeted by a long silence. Everyone including Lord Brahma looked dejected. After a long time spent pondering the matter, Lord Brahma spoke up again.

'Come, let us all go to Vaikuntha, the abode of Lord Vishnu, the Preserver of the Universe. He is the only one among all of us who can come up with a plan to help us fight Mahishasura and end his evil menace. Lord Shiva, the Great Destroyer, will be there as well. Indeed, we must not waste any more time.'

And so the unhappy gods, lured by a single ray of hope, followed Lord Indra and Lord Brahma to Vaikuntha. Lord Vishnu's abode was far, far away, but they finally reached.

Vaikuntha was a remarkable place and it rested on the massive coils of the mighty snake, Sheshanaga. The all-knowing Lord Vishnu was expecting the gods, but he did not expect to see them in such a pitiful state. In fact the great Preserver of the Universe was quite moved when he saw how dejected and hopeless the gods looked.

'Please intervene, O mighty Vishnu, Preserver of the Universe and our Protector. We need your help to fight Mahishasura, and to win back Heaven. Otherwise, this *asura* will unleash a reign of terror all across the universe and all the good things we know of—peace, justice and truth—will be lost forever.'

Lord Shiva heard these words too and quivered with rage. Lord Vishnu's face was set in stern lines and Lord Brahma looked impassive. The other gods looked agitated, disturbed and defeated.

'We must think hard,' said Lord Vishnu. 'It would be pointless frittering away our anger. If we have to do something about Mahishasura, we must think as one and focus all our energy and powers on one goal.'

The gods realised the truth behind Lord Vishnu's words. Mahishasura was no ordinary *asura*. He was a tyrannical king, but his powers were unparalleled and awe-inspiring and this made him even more of a terror. Besides, Lord Brahma's boon had made him near invincible. It would truly be an exceptional being who

could humble and kill Mahishasura, yet not destroy the sanctity of Lord Brahma's boon.

They closed their eyes and thought hard, concentrating their energies on finding a solution. The universe seemed to stop as they meditated. Every sound died away, the wind too was silenced as Vayu, the Wind God, joined the group. The ocean waters ran still as they reached the shore, for Varuna, the God of the Ocean, was deep in thought.

The gods began by examining the exact wording of Lord Brahma's boon. From that they gleaned that the being that could kill Mahishasura had to be someone who combined the special powers of every god without being a man, or a god. It was only such a being who could thwart Lord Brahma's boon. However, neither did such a divine being exist and nor could one be conjured up for the purpose.

After much debate and discussion, the *trimurti,* or the divine trinity decided that a very special goddess had to be created for the task at hand. She would have to have unique strengths and abilities and all of this required immense patience, powers of concentration and dedication.

CHAPTER FIVE

THE INVINCIBLE GODDESS

As the gods gathered around the divine trinity of Lord Brahma, Lord Vishnu and Lord Shiva, something strange happened.

Each of the gods used their respective energies to send forth a beam of light. The three beams of light came out of their raised palms to merge at a point in the centre. This combined beam of light was broader than any of the individual beams and it spread all the way across the universe. It drew on the power of all the gods present and lit up the sky like a magnificent bolt of lightning. From amidst that blinding effulgence of

light, there was a sound like that of thunder and the earth cracking. Suddenly from that fount of light and sound, there emerged a radiant goddess.

This was the Goddess Durga, who symbolised *shakti*, or the power that lay in every god. This power was scattered in the universe and was responsible for the elemental cycle of creation, preservation and destruction, that repeated itself over and over again in order to propagate life. The name Durga is a Sanskrit term for someone who cannot be vanquished and thus remains invincible.

This radiant goddess, the mighty Durga, her light scattering in every direction, appeared as a tall mountain of fire. The dispossessed gods were awed and stunned by her supreme energy and enchanting beauty. Some of them even shrank back, full of fear and awe at her majestic appearance and fiery countenance.

Her appearance was truly magnificent and grand, defying all description. Her face had the remarkable *tej*, or sublime glow that emanated from Lord Shiva. Her hair that promised to retain its lustre even in darkness was a gift from Lord Yama. Her ten arms that would soon be armed with every possible weapon of destruction, were shaped by Lord Vishnu's divine light. Her legs which could ride effortlessly through the sky, air and even in sheer emptiness, came from the energy of Lord Varuna. Her strong feet were shaped by Lord Brahma, and with them she could stand on the three known worlds and they would feel her weight only very lightly.

The gentle morning rays of Surya, the Sun God were there in her toes. Her fingers that could fight, bless devotees and play divine instruments with equal ease, were a creation of the eight gods known as the Vasus, the Nature Gods. Her nose came from the powers of Lord Kubera, the God of Wealth. The list was endless.

The gods, it seemed, had done all they could to create the most powerful divinity there ever was. And they rejoiced, for they knew for sure that now Mahishasura's days were numbered. They were also thrilled by the fact that having acted in unison, they had created this mighty Goddess, who bore a mark of all their combined energies.

There is another story which describes how the birth of Goddess Durga was foretold by a great sage. When Mahisha was a young *asura*, he was very mischievous. One day, in a spurt of madness, he disturbed the meditation of sage Raudrasva, a pupil of the great sage Katyayana. Mahishasura assumed the form of a beautiful woman and tempted Raudrasva. The young *asura* succeeded in distracting the sage and broke his penance.

A furious Katyayana then cursed Mahishasura, saying that since he took the form of a woman to cause this mischief, he would one day meet his death at the hands of a woman. The sage also mentioned that this would be no ordinary woman, but the greatest goddess that would ever be. Goddess Durga, thus born from the confluence of the powers emanating from the gods, also came to be known as Katyayani.

Emerging from the beam of light and fire, Goddess Durga spoke in a voice that resounded across the skies, assuaging and comforting all those who heard her. 'I am the same power that has shaped this universe. And now your combined forces have brought me into being so that I can save the universe from a great threat. I am here to end the menace of this evil *asura* called Mahishasura.'

Resplendent and fiery, her ten arms spread wide, almost reaching out to cover the entire sky, Durga seemed eager to set out on the task of subduing and killing Mahishasura. The gods heaped praise on her, sang verses in her glory and one by one gave her the gift of weapons that would enable her to destroy Mahishasura.

Lord Shiva gave her his *trishul,* or trident, with which he roamed the entire world. Lord Vishnu gave her his *sudarshan chakra,* or the rotating disc, that he wielded on the little finger of his hand. Lord Varuna gave her the finest conch shell the ocean waters had ever produced and a deadly noose that caught its victim by the neck in an inexorable death grip. Lord Agni handed her a missile that had the power to create devastating fires when unleashed. She had Vajra, Lord Indra's priceless thunderbolt, and Kamandalu, Lord Brahma's divine vessel.

Other gods gave her things that were symbolic of their unique powers. Lord Indra also gave her the bell that was tied around his precious white elephant called Airavata. Lord Yama, the God of Death, gifted her his staff. Lord Surya, bestowed his own rays to give her skin a lovely lustre and Kala, the God of Time, gave her a powerful sword and a shield. Lord Brahma gave her the special Akchamala—a beaded garland made of pearls, bones, dried seeds, berries, and could be embedded with a skull or two as well.

She had Lord Kubera's fine gem-studded necklace called Ratnahar. Lord Vayu gave her a bow and a quiver full of arrows that would fly swifter than the fastest winds. Lord Viswakarma, the Divine Architect, handed her a sharp axe and magical armour that could be penetrated with great difficulty. Lord Himalaya, God of the Mountains, gave her a most magnificent and fierce lion so she could ride him into the great battle against Mahishasura.

Goddess Durga also had the moon crescent over her head, symbolising Lord Shiva, for she was also an embodiment of Parvati, the invincible goddess who was Lord Shiva's consort. Beautiful rings embedded with precious stones adorned her fingers. Dhanadhipa, God of Wealth, gave her a golden vase filled with fine wine, which would fortify her during battle. Sheshanaga, the king of snakes, gave her a necklace of precious ornaments and gems, for only snakes know where the world's most precious stones are kept hidden.

Thus, equipped with fearsome weaponry and all kinds of divine powers, Goddess Durga rode off on her lion. She blew on her conch-shell repeatedly, and the lion that was her *vahana*, emitted fearsome roars that shook the three worlds.

The skies reverberated with these sounds and oceans swelled up to scrape the skies as their waters trembled and stirred violently. Entire continents were torn apart. Whole new chains of mountains rose, while older ranges crumbled, cracked, and gave way to dust in a thousand landslides. The sight of these cataclysmic changes struck terror in the hearts of all the *asuras* who watched fearfully, wondering what was to come.

But the gods rejoiced, as did the holy men, the sages and the ordinary men on the earth. As Goddess Durga rode out, she chanted verses of war and victory, and the whole universe stilled at the sound of her voice.

CHAPTER SIX

THE BEGINNING OF THE END

As Goddess Durga marched towards Heaven now ruled by Mahishasura, the *asuras* quailed in fear. They were caught completely unawares by the sight of this new enemy. They had believed that their king was invincible and there was no god, or *asura*, or man alive who could challenge him. Yet, here was someone challenging their king right at his doorstep.

The combined sounds of the lion's roars and the conch shell confused them. Believing that they were the undisputed victors of the Heaven, they initially ignored it, but the lion's roars seemed undiminished, and the sound of the conch shell resounded across the universe and made the *asuras*' ears tingle. Finally Mahishasura spoke up over the din and the clamour. 'What is that roar? Who is blowing the conch shell so very loudly? Whoever it is, must be a fool as he has no idea of my strength and power!'

Almost as an immediate response, Durga appeared in front of him. She filled up the entire sky, her radiance

even diminishing that of the sun. Her arms stretched right across to cover almost the entire universe and when she spoke, her voice struck deep fear in the hearts of most *asuras*. Only Mahishasura tried to appear undaunted.

The Goddess advanced and with every step she took, her feet left permanent hollows, deep as craters, in the ground. She twanged on the bowstring that Lord Vayu had given her, and the sound was like a low, deep, unending rumble, seeming to come from the bowels of the underworld.

Mahishasura recalled the boon granted by Lord Brahma and looking at Durga, he realized that the Goddess striding effortlessly across the skies had come to destroy him. But his power had made him arrogant and fearless. He refused to accept defeat and stubbornly commanded his *asura* warriors to prepare for battle.

Another story tells how Mahishasura was prodded into action by Narada, the celestial saint, whose other role was that of the eternal mischief-maker. Goddess Durga came down to reside in the ancient mountain range known as the Vindhyas and Narada extolled her uncommon and extraordinary beauty in great measure to the *asura* king.

Terribly smitten by all that he heard, the *asura* sent her a proposal of marriage. The one thing good about Mahishasura was that he was direct and honest. He told her of his origins and the asked for her hand. The Goddess seeing this as the perfect opportunity to defeat the *asura*, came up with a plan. She refused his proposal saying that she would only accept a consort who could defeat her in battle.

Deeply humiliated that his proposal was turned down so easily by the Goddess, Mahishasura accepted this challenge and accordingly sent in his best generals to fight her.

In the first instance, Mahishasura sent his general Chiksura to lead the *asuras* into battle. Chiksura was tall, immensely strong, with cheeks that bulged out and horns that curved like serpents over his head. He was so powerful and fear-inspiring that a single look could send enemy soldiers scuttling away like ants. The *asuras* were a sight to see, frothing at the mouth and their eyes red-rimmed with the excitement of the battle at hand. As they charged forward, their hoarse shouts mingled with the trumpeting of their elephants, the shrill neighing of the horses and the deafening sounds of chariots being driven furiously onto the battlefield.

Goddess Durga watched them come and blew furiously. Gale-like winds of great strength blew hither and thither, scattering away half of the powerful *asura* army. She then stretched out her sword, and proceeded to strike down several thousand of the remaining *asuras*.

She then picked up her bow and aimed arrows that flew out like an unending shower, one after another. Her aim was so unerring, and the power of her arrows so divine, that severed heads lolled on the battlefield within moments of her unleashing those arrows. The lion on which she rode, not to be outdone, roared ever

more furiously and mauled several retreating *asuras* and killed them instantly.

Then the Goddess exhaled deeply and hundreds of thousands of warriors appeared as if by magic. They were known as the *ganas*. They were dressed in armour that shone as it caught the light of the sun. They marched in an orderly, disciplined manner, each one of them equipped with weapons of war. The *ganas* wielded clubs, maces, bows and arrows, the scimitar, the axe, and at one single command from the Goddess, proceeded to wreak havoc on the *asura* army. They blew on their conch shells and beat their drums and trumpets, making the *asuras* even more wary and fearful. Some of them even dropped their weapons and ran for dear life.

In mere moments, the immense and mighty army of *asuras* that Mahishasura was so proud of, was reduced to shambles. The gods watching the battle scene from a distance, showered fragrant flowers on the Goddess Durga and her army of warriors. They now knew for a fact that Mahishasura's days were numbered.

Seeing his army scattered and most of his soldiers dead or injured, the mighty Chiksura could hold back his anger no more. 'Oh cowards,' he cried, and his voice was like the very roar of a mountain lion. Hearing this sound, Goddess Durga's lion roared even louder in indignation. 'Why, you are supposed to be brave soldiers, the best in the three worlds. And look at you now, running scared like frightened birds! Don't tell me you cannot fight against an army led by a woman, when we have already vanquished the gods and driven them out of Heaven?'

Hearing Chiksura call out thus, Durga now took on the form of Ambika. She was able to create other goddesses out of herself, each one bearing different powers. Ambika aimed a gust of arrows at the *asura* general. Soon his steed lay dead on the field of battle, and his charioteer too slumped to the ground. When Chiksura took up his bow, he found himself stretching a broken string, for the Goddess was faster than him. Enraged and cursing loudly, he rushed towards the Goddess, sword in hand. He thrust out at her lion, and aimed for the Goddess' right hand. But the moment it neared her, the sword broke in half. And then, Ambika picked up her trident and aimed it straight and unerringly at the *asura* and he was killed instantly.

Seeing their general dead, another of Mahishasura's trusted *asura* warriors called Chamara took command of the army and led them out into battle. The *asuras* looked very nervous and uncertain as they followed their leader. The *ganas* laughed heartily at this sight. They were determined to humiliate and defeat the *asuras*.

Chamara aimed the lethal weapon called Shakti at the Goddess, but she absorbed it calmly. After all, it was fashioned from the same power that had created her. Chamara then sent another powerful weapon towards her, but she cut it to pieces with the swift arrows that flew from her bow one after the other.

Seeing Chamara advance on his elephant, the Goddess' lion leaped high and landed sharply on the elephant's forehead. As the elephant bent down, Chamara was forced to jump to the ground, and

there followed a fierce duel between the *asura* and the Goddess. But it was a duel that did not last long. With a powerful swipe of her sword, she severed Chamara's head from his body, and for long moments, it lay on the ground, the tongue lolling out, thirsty for water.

Several other *asuras* such as Udagra, Karala, Uddhata, Baskala, Ugrasya, Mahahanu, Bidala and Durmukha appeared in turn to take on the Goddess Durga, but she ground each one of them to dust with her mace, or killed them with her arrows, club, trident, or sword. The *asuras* now had no choice but to turn to their king, Mahishasura.

CHAPTER SEVEN

THE GREATEST BATTLE

Mahishasura, hearing of the Goddess' destruction of his armies and the murder of his generals, was struck by a strange fear. He remembered the sage Katyayan's curse. For a brief moment he thought of running away too, but then dismissed the cowardly notion as he was a valiant warrior.

He heard Durga's taunts and her repeated challenges to his soldiers who could not really put up any kind of effective resistance to her. So he charged into battle himself. He once again assumed his buffalo form, for this had worked to his advantage in earlier battles, usually with devastating results for the enemy.

Mahishasura first attacked the soldiers of the Goddess. Some he gored with his horns, so that they bled to death. Others, he kicked with his hooves, so that they were crushed like powder. Some others were singed by his fiery breath.

He lashed out wildly with his tail, and its force was such that limbs of those who came near were severed instantly. The Goddess' lion seeing the buffalo wreak such rampant destruction around him, now roared furiously and jumped towards Mahishasura.

As the lion and the buffalo demon grappled with each other, the Goddess seized the initiative. She threw

the deadly noose, grabbing the buffalo by the neck. She struck at him with her sword, but Mahishasura slipped out of the noose by changing his form. Next, he turned into an elephant and with his huge looping trunk, pulled the Goddess' lion towards him. The Goddess chopped off his trunk with her sword. Then he became a lion, but Durga deftly sliced off its head.

As the battle raged, the Goddess stopped to drink a bit of the wine that lay stored in the vessel that had been granted to her. The demon danced around her, changing shape and taunting her all the while. But the Goddess only smiled at his efforts. 'Shout all you will, you puny *asura*,' she thought to herself. 'Once I am done with my wine, I will destroy you like I have all the other *asuras*.'

Then she jumped onto the buffalo demon and raising her sword high over Mahishasura, she sliced off the buffalo head. As the demon began to emerge in his real form from the buffalo's severed neck, the Goddess laughed heartily once again, mocking all of Mahishasura's efforts to scare her. Then before he could fully emerge as an *asura*, she had placed her foot on his neck and killed him, her trident piercing him deep in the chest and her sword cutting his head off with a powerful stroke.

With a horrifying groan, Mahishasura fell to the ground like a giant uprooted tree, crushing hundreds of *asuras* under him. Seeing their commander and leader destroyed, the army cried out in confusion and were soon driven to defeat.

In another version of this story, Mahishasura was able to revive himself three times and every time the

Goddess assumed different forms to kill him. She took on the fearful incarnations of Ugrachandi and Bhadrakali. Finally, she appeared as Durga and killed the *asura* king.

However, the interesting thing is that Mahishasura was truly in awe of the Goddess and had worshipped her since he had come to know that he would meet his end at her hands.

Near the final moments of battle, he insisted that he would willingly die at her hands, but he would never be detached from Goddess Durga. And this is why, after the buffalo demon is finally killed by the third incarnation of the Goddess, all images show Durga along with Mahishasura, frozen in his moment of final defeat, impaled by Durga's spear and crushed beneath her left foot. The Goddess and the demon are always shown together and that is how they are worshipped to this very day.

Seeing the destruction of the *asura* who had tormented them, and made their lives miserable, the gods were loud and lavish in their praises of the Goddess. They bowed in devotion and reverence to her. Sages chanted holy verses and the demi-gods called the *gandharvas*, sang songs of praise. 'O Devi, how can we describe your abundant valour and wonderful feats in battle?' they sang. 'To that Ambika who is worthy of worship by all *devas* and sages and who pervades this world by her supreme power, we bow in devotion. May you grant us auspicious things and always protect the universe from evil!'

So the chants and songs in Goddess Durga's honour continued.

And indeed, whenever they were in trouble, Goddess Durga would ride out to rescue them, time and time

again. For killing the *asura*, the goddess Durga is also called 'Mahishamardini' or the killer of Mahisha the demon. And as a reward for all her soldiers who had fought so bravely, the goddess bestowed on them the boon to be able to make the finest jewellery. Thereafter her ganas were known as the *sonaras* or jewellers.

It is believed that the battle with Mahishasura and his army of demons took ten cosmic days. On the tenth day, when he was finally vanquished, Durga's victory was celebrated as Vijaya Dashami, marking the triumph of good over evil.

In later times, the Goddess would take on other forms to kill all the other *asuras* who were followers and children of Mahishasura. She assumed the form of Kali, when the time came for the evil *asura* Raktabhija to be killed. He had been granted the boon that from every drop of his blood that spilled to the ground, other Raktabhijas would emerge. The Goddess Kali licked away these drops of blood before they fell to the earth and in the end, killed Raktabhija himself.

As Chandika or Kaushiki, she destroyed the evil *asura* brothers called Chand-Mund and as Gauri, she killed two other *asuras* Shumbha and Nishumbha.

MythNotes

The battle with Mahishasura continued over ten cosmic days and culminates in the actual slaying which is on Vijaya Dashami. This is celebrated as Durga Puja in Bengal and Navratri in most other parts of India, especially in Gujarat. The practice of worshipping Durga in autumn is believed to have begun from the time when the exiled King Rama, who was searching for his wife Sita, offered prayers, seeking the Goddess Durga's blessings. The festival of Dussehra coincides with Vijaya Dashami marks the victory of Rama over Ravana.

Images of Durga as Mahishamardini appear as sculptures throughout India's early history. The museum in Mathura has a statue of the Goddess with six arms. This dates back to the 2nd century BC. *It is however more than 500 years later, when the imperial Guptas ruled over large parts of north India, that some of the finest sculptures of Mahishasuramardini, or the slaying of the demon, appear. In most of these statues, the Goddess is shown armed with a spear and a trident. In the far south, in Mamallapuram, a relief sculpture of the Goddess depicts her with eight arms. She is shown astride a lion, fighting the half-buffalo half-demon Mahishasura. A similar sculpture also appears in the cave temples of Ellora.*

Mahishasura's kingdom called Mahisha, or Mahishaka is believed to be the present-day city of Mysore in Karnataka.